Divorce

RESOURCES FOR BIBLICAL LIVING

Divorce

Before You Say "I Don't"

LOU PRIOLO

P&R PUBLISHING
P.O. BOX 817 • PHILLIPSBURG • NEW JERSEY 08865-0817

Unless otherwise indicated, Scripture quotations are from the NEW AMERICAN STANDARD BIBLE®. Copyright © 1960, 1962, 1963, 1968, 1971, 1972, 1973, 1975, 1977, 1995 by The Lockman Foundation. Used by permission.

Italics within Scripture quotations indicate emphasis added.

Some material in this booklet has been adapted from chapter 14 of *The Complete Husband*, published by Calvary Press. Used by permission. For more information, visit www.calvarypress.com.

The material in the appendix has been adapted from *Losing That Lovin' Feeling*, pages 213–18, available from Pastoral Publications (2003). Used by permission.

Box graphic © www.istockphoto.com

Printed in the United States of America

Library of Congress Cataloging-in-Publication Data

Priolo, Lou.
Divorce : before you say "I don't" / Lou Priolo.
   p. cm. — (Resources for biblical living)
ISBN-13: 978-1-59638-078-3 (pbk.)
1. Divorce—Religious aspects—Christianity. 2. Divorce—Biblical teaching. I. Title.
BT707.P75 2007
248.8'46—dc22

               2007029746

Marriage is a very difficult thing to get out of without sinning. And the fact is, sin has its consequence—misery.

> Do not be deceived, God is not mocked; for whatever a man sows, this he will also reap. For the one who sows to his own flesh will from the flesh reap corruption, but the one who sows to the Spirit will from the Spirit reap eternal life. Let us not lose heart in doing good, for in due time we will reap if we do not grow weary. (Gal. 6:7–9)

The purpose of this booklet is twofold: first, to help inform you of the misery associated with initiating an unbiblical divorce; and second, to persuade you not to "lose heart in doing" what is "good" for your family (and what will most glorify God).

Now, perhaps your mind is made up, and there is little I can do to persuade you to reevaluate your course of action. But please, at least be willing to hear me out so that before you squeeze the trigger, you will be certain of what you are in for. Besides, it will take me only a few short pages to make my case. Your future happiness is certainly worth a small investment of your time.

Now, I know that my manner of writing is very direct. All right, it's downright "in your face." But you see, as a biblical counselor with over twenty-three years' experience in trying to save marriages, I know all too well the misery you will be facing if you pursue a divorce on less than biblical grounds. In all my years of counseling, I do not recall even one Christian who has not suffered tremendously for making the decision you are contemplating. Most of them have come back in one way or another and acknowledged that the suffering they experienced was much greater than they had initially thought it would be. More significantly, they invariably told me that if they had to do it over again, they wouldn't. So please be tolerant of my desperate plea to keep you from falling off a very high cliff.

If you haven't yet closed the book (or thrown it against the wall), thank you.

"You're welcome. But what of all this misery you promised me?"

I can't cover in this booklet *all* the consequences you are likely to experience, but I will do what I can in the allotted time. Let's be clear about one thing, though: I'm not the one promising the consequences—God is!

To begin with, if you initiate an unbiblical divorce, *you will be confirming to all your brothers and sisters in Christ that you have a hard heart.*

> Some Pharisees came to Jesus, testing Him and asking, "Is it lawful for a man to divorce his wife for any reason at all?" And He answered and said, "Have you not read that He who created them from the beginning made them male and female, and said, 'For this reason a man shall leave his father and mother and be joined to his wife, and the two shall become one flesh'? So they are no longer two, but one flesh. What therefore God has joined together, let no man separate." They said to Him, "Why then did Moses command to give her a certificate of divorce and send her away?" He said to them, "*Because of your hardness of heart Moses permitted you to divorce your wives*; but from the beginning it has not been this way. And I say to you, whoever divorces his wife, except for immorality, and marries another woman commits adultery." (Matt. 19:3–9)

When a Christian initiates an unbiblical divorce, it's *always* because he has hardened his heart against God.[1]

---

1. And I daresay that it is *always* because someone is influencing him to do so. Chances are excellent that someone in your life is influencing your thinking in this

Some time ago, I was in my office, trying to convince a woman that she didn't have biblical justification for the divorce she was seeking. No matter how hard I tried to get her to look at what the Scriptures teach, she wouldn't be persuaded. As I began pressing home the Scriptures, trying to convict her with them, she seemed to be impervious to them. Although I was throwing everything in the Book at her, she seemed impenetrable. I couldn't get the truth of God's Word around the roadblocks she had set up in her heart. Finally, she tried to justify her sinful plans by saying, "You don't know my heart. Only God does, and He understands." To which I responded, "You are right about that. God *does* know your heart, and He understands that it's *hard!*"

And hardness of heart is a very serious thing. To be hard-hearted is to willfully and stubbornly refuse to do what God tells you to do. Like Pharaoh, who was determined to do things his way, a hard-hearted person will not listen to God. And as He did with Pharaoh, God will see to it that He is not mocked.

Next, there is the fact that *you will bring shame to the name of Christ* by your divorce. Rather than glorifying God by learning how to suffer for righteousness (let alone learning how to turn your difficult marriage around), you will do exactly the opposite—you will bring reproach to His name. As Nathan the prophet explained to David after David had committed adultery with Bathsheba and tried to cover it up by having her husband Uriah the Hittite killed, "by this deed you have given occasion to the enemies of the LORD to blaspheme" (2 Sam. 12:14; see Rom. 2:24). Your divorce will be a public testimony to the fact that Jesus Christ and the Word of God do not have what it takes to help people solve their problems without sinning.

> You who boast in the Law, through your breaking the Law,
> do you dishonor God? For "the name of God is blasphemed

---

area in one way or another. Have you considered the extent to which such a person is giving you biblical advice?

among the Gentiles because of you," just as it is written. (Rom. 2:23–24)

You will be subject to God's discipline. For the disobedient Christian, discipline is certain! "For those whom the Lord loves He disciplines, and He scourges every son whom He receives" (Heb. 12:6).

You shouldn't expect God to bless your disobedience by removing all the natural (and supernatural) consequences of your sin. It doesn't matter how miserable you think you are in your current circumstances. If you pursue this divorce, in the long run you will be even more miserable than you are now, though you *may* seemingly experience some momentary relief from your suffering. But even this is unlikely. The Bible declares, "The way of the treacherous is hard" (Prov. 13:15).

And if you attend a church that practices biblical discipline, you will place your spiritual leaders in a position of being compelled to deal with your sin in a potentially public manner. Of course, this will actually be a good thing for you. But being removed from the provision and protection of the church, not to mention being delivered over to Satan (cf. 1 Cor. 5:5), will not be a pleasant experience.

The next consequence worth considering is that *you will multiply your misery by the guilt and bitterness you will inevitably experience.* Someone has likened depression to the physical exhaustion that occurs when an individual exercises too long. Overexerting yourself during physical exercise will ultimately result in a temporary depletion of strength and vigor. Running around the track a few too many times, for example, will eventually sap your physical energy and cause you to become physically exhausted. Similarly, living day in and day out with guilt over sin that has not been properly confessed and forsaken expends a certain amount of emotional energy; it saps your emotional strength and causes you to become emotionally exhausted (i.e., depressed).

Bitterness (or resentment) is the result of an unwilling-ness to properly forgive those who have sinned against you.[2] It requires emotional energy to maintain such a grudge. Resent-ment, like guilt, will deplete your energy if allowed to reside in your heart too long. Remember, too, that after a divorce, the potential for resentment will be greater as a result of additional hurts that will occur between now and then.

One more thing—if you go through with this, you may also find your bitterness increasing as you try to assuage your guilt by constantly reminding yourself of how bad your spouse was (and why, in light of all your spouse's faults, you are justified in breaking your marriage vows). In other words, if you try to balance your guilt with blame by reminding yourself of your ex's sins and foibles, you will grow bitter.

The last consequence I would like you to think about is the fact that *you will cause much hurt and potential harm to others.* The person you are thinking of abandoning will be wounded in all sorts of ways. He or she will have to deal not only with the loss of your companionship (feeble as you might think that has been lately) but also with a loss of emotional support, comfort, security, and reputation. He or she will be exposed to an entirely new level of fear, anger, bitterness, loneliness, anxiety, depres-sion, and sorrow. And you will be largely responsible for your spouse's additional misery.

Now, what about the hurt and misery that a divorce will bring to your children? Chances are, this is the one consequence you have thought about more than any other because, after all, you do love your children. And I daresay that it has probably been for the sake of the children that you have not seriously contem-plated getting a divorce any sooner. By this time, perhaps you have even convinced yourself that your children will be better off

2. And please don't fool yourself into thinking that you can forgive your spouse and then turn around and divorce him or her unbiblically. You can't have it both ways. Either you truly forgive your spouse and seek reconciliation or you refuse to reconcile and don't forgive biblically.

having two parents who are separated but "at peace" with each other than having parents who are together but at each other's throats all the time. Well, have you asked them? I mean, have you sat down with them and, in all sincerity, asked them how they believe their lives will be impacted by a divorce? Please don't sign those papers without first doing that. I could fill the rest of this booklet, as well as many others, with stories of children I've known whose parents' divorces have caused them more misery than their parents ever imagined. I know of family members who, to this day, are estranged from one another because of divorce. But this would probably not convince you to reconsider your course of action nearly as much as if your own children told you personally how they believe a divorce would impact their young lives. Even if your children are married or gone from your home, I urge you to ask them how they believe a divorce would affect them. The answers might just surprise you.

If you think this conversation will be too difficult to handle right now, imagine having it five or ten years from now when, with tears in their eyes, your children recount for you not potentially painful scenarios that have yet to occur, but actual gut-wrenching, agonizing accounts of how your selfishness has produced consequences in their lives from which they have yet to fully recover.

"But you are making me out to be the 'bad guy' and my spouse to be the 'good guy.'"

No one is the good guy in marriage, for we are all sinners. You got married knowing that your spouse was a sinner. You promised to stay married in spite of his or her frailties. Listen to what Puritan pastor Richard Baxter said over three hundred years ago about the condition of you and your spouse:

> Remember still that you are both diseased persons, full of infirmities; and therefore expect the fruit of those infirmities in each other; and make not a strange matter of it, as if you had never known of it before. If you had married one that is lame,

would you be angry at her for halting [limping]? Or if you had married one that had a putrid ulcer, would you fall out with her because it stinketh? Did you not know beforehand, that you married a person of such weakness, as would yield you some manner of daily trial and offense? If you could not bear this, you should not have married her; if you resolved that you could bear it then, you are obliged to bear it now. Resolve therefore to bear with one another; as remembering that you took one another as sinful, frail, imperfect persons, not as angels, or as blameless and perfect.[3]

Space will not permit me to unpack many of the other consequences of divorce. Suffice it to say that divorce is the gift that keeps on giving. It will continue to bring misery both to you and to those you profess to love for years and perhaps generations to come.

"All right, I know it is a sin for me to initiate this divorce and that there may be consequences, but I also know that God will forgive me."

Let's think this through for a moment. Suppose you were the president of a bank and I walked into your office one day with a somber look on my face.

"Do you remember when your bank was robbed three weeks ago?" I ask you.

"I certainly do," you reply with a suspicious tone in your voice and look in your eye.

"Well, I don't know how to say this exactly, but . . . well, uh, I'm here to confess to the crime and beg you to forgive me. I'm really, *really* sorry. Look, I know I don't deserve it, but do you think you could find it in your heart to forgive me? Please?"

"I see. Well, where's the money you stole?"

"Money?"

"Yeah, I really would like to have my money back."

---

3. Richard Baxter, *The Christian Directory* (Ligonier, PA: Soli Deo Gloria, 1997), 433 (clarification added).

"But I came to ask you to *forgive* me. I really don't want to return the money. Can't you just forgive me and forget about the money?"

"Of course not! You've got to be willing to make restitution before I can even consider granting forgiveness to you."

Do you see how foolish it is for you to expect God to forgive your sinful divorce without your first being willing to repent and, if possible, reconcile with your spouse?

"But what if I just can't live with that person any longer? I really think I'll go crazy if I have to stay married to him [or her]; besides, I just can't believe that God wants me to stay in an unhappy marriage."

So what you are telling me is that you feel trapped—sort of like you are in a box. And with every day that goes by, the box seems to become more unbearable. You have convinced yourself that the box is shrinking and that you will soon be crushed by the ever-tightening walls. You are becoming claustrophobic and feel as though you are suffocating. Is that about right?

"Pretty much!"

Okay, so here you are in the box. You're cramped, uncomfortable, and becoming more frustrated with each passing hour. You want the pressure you're feeling to be lifted so that you can have some relief. You want to get out of the box for good!

"You've got it."

The Bible has some very important things to say to you about that box. In 1 Corinthians 10:13, the apostle Paul says, "No temptation has overtaken you but such as is common to man; and God is faithful, who will not allow you to be tempted beyond what you are able, but with the temptation will provide the way of escape also, so that you will be able to endure it."

The first thing God wants you to know is that you're not the only one who has ever been encased in the kind of box you're in. Your trouble isn't new. It is "common to man." That is, although it may have a few unique components, it is nonetheless a kind of trouble, or box, that has imprisoned many others before you.

Indeed, there are others (even other Christians) who are basically in the same box as you are right now. You are certainly not the only Christian who has had a troubled marriage!

Another thing that God tells you about your box in this verse is that He has limited the trouble you are in, and He has done that in two very important ways. He has limited your trouble in *scope*, and He has limited it in *duration*. See the figure for an illustration of this truth.

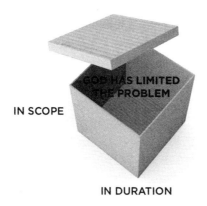

IN SCOPE

GOD HAS LIMITED THE PROBLEM

IN DURATION

God's faithfulness to you means, first of all, that He "will not allow you to be tempted beyond what you are able." That is, He will not allow the temptation to become so difficult that you will not be *able* to deal with it biblically (in a way that is not sinful and that will bring glory to God). In other words, He will not let your box become so small that it will crush or smother you!

Second, God's faithful promise to you as a Christian is that your trial will come to an end. He will "provide the way of escape . . . , so that you will be able to endure it." God promises that someday, in some way, your trial will end. He says that someday, He is going to let you out of the box.[4] He doesn't tell

4. Even those Christians who are suffering with incurable or terminal illnesses have hope that someday God will let them out of the boxes of their fleshly tents (their physical bodies) and deliver them into the freedom (cf. Rom. 8:18–22) of their heavenly homes ("a building from God, a house not made with hands, eternal in the heavens," 2 Cor. 5:1).

you *how* He's going to do it; He doesn't tell you *when*—only that He *will* do it.

Yes, sooner or later, God is going to let you out of the box. He may provide your "way of escape" by sending a bulldozer crashing through the wall. He may push a button that will silently trigger a trap door in the floor of the box. He may send a giant can opener to tear off the top of the box and throw a ladder down for you to climb out. Perhaps He will send an army of angels to march around the perimeter of your box and, after a shout, the walls will come crashing down like the walls of Jericho. He may simply snap His fingers and the entire box will disappear. But the thing I want you to understand most is that you are safer, and ultimately happier, inside the box right now than you would be outside of it. In fact, you mentioned that you thought you were going to go crazy if you had to live any longer with your spouse. The truth is, you are more likely to go crazy by stepping out of God's revealed will than you are by obeying His Word and suffering for the sake of righteousness.[5] Removing yourself from the place where the Word of God says you belong is a serious thing. "Like a bird that wanders from her nest, so is a man who wanders from his home" (Prov. 27:8). It is your self-centeredness and discontentment that is tempting you to forsake your spouse, hurt and separate yourself from family, seek your own desire, and look for greener pastures elsewhere.[6]

The question I want to ask as you contemplate your box is this: Are you going to cooperate with God's plan to get you out of the box of this miserable marriage, or are you going to impatiently pull out your sinful little pocketknife and attempt to tunnel your way out of the box before God, through righteous means, extricates you in His own way?

---

5. Many Christians seem to have forgotten, if they ever knew in the first place, that part of the package that comes when we were signed up for biblical Christianity is the suffering to which God calls us (Matt. 5:10–12; 16:24; 2 Tim. 3:12; 1 Peter 2:19–25). Sometimes that suffering comes in the form of having to endure a difficult marriage.

6. Cf. Prov. 18:1.

"How can I cooperate with His plan?"

For starters, you can ask yourself this question: What might the Lord be preparing me for while I am in the box?

"Why do you want me to think about that?"

I want you to ponder that question because as long as you stay put in the box, He is readying you for something that He has prepared for you when He is ready to let you out.

"Okay, so what might He be preparing for me if I stay put?"

Although you do not know what the future holds, the Bible identifies some of the things that God often does as a result of trials and tribulations—provided, of course, that you submit yourself to His agenda.

You can be certain of one thing. You will be a lot happier if, in order to glorify God, you decide to abandon your plans to pursue this unbiblical divorce instead of rebelliously walking out on His revealed will for your life.

"How can you know that I will not be happier if I leave? That sounds presumptuous, if you ask me!"

I can say it because happiness is ultimately a direct result of obedience to Scripture. Jesus said, "Blessed [or *happy*] are those who hear the word of God and observe it" (Luke 11:28). As you and I become conformed to the image of Christ, we become better equipped to biblically handle the trials of life and consequently experience greater joy, peace, and happiness in the midst of them. The more you become conformed to the image of Christ as a result of biblically responding to trials, the more those sinful patterns that the Bible says produce misery will be removed from your life. The degree of misery will be replaced with the same degree of happiness. As Peter put it, "He who has suffered in the flesh has ceased from sin, so as to live the rest of the time in the flesh no longer for the lusts of men, but for the will of God" (1 Peter 4:1b–2). The more you live for God's will rather than for your own desires, the greater will be your measure of happiness.

15

Remaining in the box will also prepare you for greater ministry.[7]

> Blessed be the God and Father of our Lord Jesus Christ, the Father of mercies and God of all comfort, who comforts us in all our affliction so that we will be able to comfort those who are in any affliction with the comfort with which we ourselves are comforted by God. (2 Cor. 1:3–4)

One of God's sovereign designs for your trials is to better prepare you to assist (*comfort*) others with the assistance that He (through the Holy Spirit) will be giving you. This may not excite you right now, but down the road, you will appreciate it as you experience the joy and satisfaction of helping others, not just with marital issues but with a variety of other problems. (The passage says that we will be better equipped "to comfort those who are in *any* affliction.")

There's also the matter of strengthening your relationship with God—learning how to better depend on Him and have fellowship with Him. Our God is a *living* God who desires to be intimately involved in our lives. He desires us to worship Him in *spirit* as well as in truth. He wants us to have fellowship with Him through prayer[8] and the Word. The more time you spend with God in the Word and prayer, the greater will be your peace, your strength, and your hope for the future. You will come to know Him better and perhaps, like Paul, know more fully "the power of His resurrection and the fellowship of His sufferings" (Phil. 3:10).

One more thing to consider about this matter: God may want to glorify Himself by restoring your marriage to a place that exceeds all your expectations so that His power will be made perfect in your weakness.

---

7. Cutting your way out of the box is likely to disqualify you from all sorts of ministry opportunities.

8. On the other hand, according to 1 Peter 3:7, your prayers are likely to be hindered if you don't relate to your spouse honorably.

"But I don't think my spouse is really a Christian. And I know the Lord doesn't want me to be unequally yoked to an unbeliever."

The verse to which you are alluding, 2 Corinthians 6:14, is at best a *premarital counseling* verse. The verse you should be looking at now that you are married is 1 Corinthians 7:11: "The husband should not divorce his wife."

You may not divorce your spouse even if she (or he) is an unbeliever: "If any brother has a wife who is an unbeliever, and she consents to live with him, he must not divorce her" (1 Cor. 7:12).[9] Besides, if your spouse is a member in good standing of a Bible-believing church, she is considered a "so-called brother," as Paul put it in 1 Corinthians 5:11, and you shouldn't be talking about her as if she were a pagan—at least not until her church deals with her on the matter.

Nothing short of marital infidelity or desertion by an unbelieving spouse constitutes a biblical (i.e., nonsinful)[10] divorce. So even if you are married to a person who does not profess to be a Christian, as long as he or she is pleased to live with you, you must stay put and try to make the marriage work. Are you willing to suffer for doing what is right?[11]

"I don't know that I'm prepared to take that much suffering."

Consider the alternative. In all my years of ministry, I've never seen an unbiblical divorce cause less pain and suffering than it would have taken to fix the marriage. Oh, to be sure, it is difficult to stick it out. It requires much endurance and lots of hard work. But as hard as it is to stay married, it's much harder

---

9. A two-part cassette series entitled "Married to an Unbeliever" is available through Sound Word Associates. You may obtain a copy by calling (219) 548-0933 or by visiting http://www.soundword.com/lou-priolo-library-priolo--lou.html.

10. Although all divorce is the result of sin, not all divorces are sinful. For a more complete explanation of the traditional Protestant view of divorce, see Jay Adams, *Marriage, Divorce, and Remarriage in the Bible* (Grand Rapids: Zondervan, 1986).

11. Cf. Matt. 5:10; 1 Peter 2:19–25; 3:14–18; 4:15–17.

to pursue a sinful divorce because "the way of the unfaithful is hard" (Prov. 13:15 NKJV).

Over the years, I've heard many reasons (excuses, really) that people give to defend their decision to justify sinful divorces. They all come down to pretty much the same thing: I know this divorce is wrong, but because *my* case is different, God will make an exception. As we have seen, your case is not different, for "no temptation has overtaken you but such as is common to man" (1 Cor. 10:13a).

On the pages that follow, I have listed a few more of the many other lies that people tell themselves about why they are justified in pursuing their sinful divorces. Perhaps you have utilized a few of these false reasonings to rationalize the unbiblical divorce you are contemplating. Next to each excuse, I have provided one of several biblical counterarguments, as well as a few related Scripture passages. Let me urge you to open your Bible and consider each point before you deceive yourself in breaking the covenant you made with God.

"My feelings have changed. I've fallen out of love with her."

RELATED SCRIPTURE: Prov. 28:26; Matt. 24:12; 1 Cor. 13:5–7; Rev. 2:1–7

People "fall in love" because they want to. When you "fell in love" with your wife, you were not struck with some external force such as Cupid's arrow. Neither were you dazzled by some external influence such as Love Potion #9. The romantic feelings you enjoyed, which you claim to have now lost, were of your own making. They were created in your own heart. They, like your other feelings, are largely the result of your thoughts and ways. You "fell in love" with your spouse as a result of what you *did to, for,* and *with* her and as a result of what you *told yourself* about her. You created those romantic feelings, and by God's grace, you can make them come back.

Think for a moment about what you did when the two of you were first courting. Didn't you spend lots of time doing fun things together? Didn't you invest hour after hour revealing your heart to her and listening to her reveal her heart to you? Didn't you spend time, money, and effort doing things for her—even while you were apart? Didn't you often think about all those wonderful qualities in your sweetheart that you admired? In fact, wasn't the majority of your spare time (and even some "not so spare" time) consumed with musings about how wonderful your relationship with your special friend was? Wasn't your imagination often engaged in anticipation of spending lots of time with this person?

The totality of these mental, emotional, and behavioral investments generated those feelings that our culture equates with "falling in love." Consequently, the more you did *to, with*, and *for* the other person, and the more time you spent thinking such loving thoughts about her, the greater the potential you had to develop feelings of love. And if your spouse was doing the same kinds of loving things to, with, and for you, the feelings became even more intense. Moreover, if your relationship was relatively free of conflict and your partner was putting her "best foot forward," you may not have had enough information to balance those feelings of love with wisdom.

But now, bitterness (lack of forgiveness) has crept into your relationship and has effectively short-circuited that part of your heart that generates romantic feelings. It's basically just that simple! Get rid of the bitterness (i.e., forgive your spouse), change the way you think about and act toward her, and the romantic feelings will return. It's like the Lord said to the church at Ephesus who had "fallen out of love" with Him: "Remember from where you have fallen, and repent [change your thinking and the direction of your life] and do the deeds you did at first" (Rev. 2:5).

"That man has killed all the love I ever had for him."

RELATED SCRIPTURE: Lev. 19:18; Matt. 5:43–48; 22:34–40; Gal. 5:14; Eph. 5:25; Titus 2:3–5

If you are telling me that you no longer love your spouse, you are seriously breaking the second greatest commandment, "You shall love your neighbor as yourself" (Matt. 22:39). Your husband is your closest neighbor. You share your life, your children, your home, your table, even your bed (and body). Indeed, you are "one flesh" with him (cf. Gen. 2:24).

And by not loving your spouse, you also break commands in dozens of other passages that require you to love (even your enemies).

Besides, biblical love "bears all things, believes all things, hopes all things, endures all things" (1 Cor. 13:7). Perhaps you never really did love your partner the way you should have in the first place.

If you truly are a Christian, you can learn to do whatever the Bible says you ought to do. You can certainly learn to love your (closest) neighbor.

"It is not good for the children to have to live in a home with so much conflict, hatred, and disharmony."

RELATED SCRIPTURE: Jer. 16:12; Luke 12:1; Rom. 12:18; 14:19; 1 Cor. 7:12–16; Eph. 4:3; 6:4; 1 Thess. 5:13; 1 Tim. 4:12; Heb. 12:25

No, it isn't good. But comparing the harm of living with parents who are seriously at odds to the harm of breaking their family apart is, generally speaking, like comparing catching a cold to getting double pneumonia. The effects of one are far less severe than the effects of the other.

Besides, the Bible offers help and hope for correcting these issues. "So far as it depends on you," you must "be at peace with" your spouse (Rom. 12:18). This is especially true when both of you claim to be believers in Jesus Christ. As bad as this current situation is for your children, it would almost certainly be worse for them to have to endure the demise of their family—not to mention the terrible impact that your example of selfishness, hypocrisy, and rebellion would be likely to have on them.

"I'm tired of trying."

RELATED SCRIPTURE: 1 Sam. 1:24ff.; Heb. 10:36; 12:1–11; James 1:2–8

The Bible says, "You have need of endurance, so that when you have done the will of God [probably not for days or weeks, but after you have done the will of God day and night for months or years], you may receive what was promised" (Heb. 10:36). Endurance is the ability to weather a trial without resorting to sinful means of deliverance—like this divorce you are contemplating. An enduring person has the ability to keep a biblical perspective about his troubles by not magnifying a tolerable trial so that it appears to his mind to be an intolerable one. Chances are, the difficulties you are going through that tempt you to throw in the towel on your marriage are not nearly as intolerable as you imagine. Sure, they are painful, but you must be careful not to feel a flesh wound as though it were a knife through the heart. You will also do well to consider that God may be using the trials in your marriage to chastise you and sanctify you for your own good and for His glory. And if you think you are being "spanked" rather severely right now, how much more severely do you suppose you will be chastised after this sinful divorce?

"I have peace about it."

RELATED SCRIPTURE: Jonah 1:5–6; Rom. 14:22–23; Col. 3:15

So did Jonah. He apparently had so much peace about running away from God's will that he fell asleep in the belly of the ship in the midst of a violent storm. Peaceful feelings can be deceptive. Besides, having peace is never mentioned in the Bible as a way of determining God's will. For that, we must consult God's Word—which is clear about this matter.

"He has lied to me repeatedly.
I will never be able to trust him again."

RELATED SCRIPTURE: Prov. 3:5–6; 20:6, Luke 17:3; Acts 15:36–39; Col. 4:10; 2 Tim. 4:11; 1 Peter 3:5–6

Where is it written that you must trust your spouse to stay married to him? Consider Sarah, who the Bible says trusted in God while being submissive to her husband, Abraham. Besides, since your husband has asked your forgiveness, it is your responsibility to forgive him for lying. It is his responsibility to earn back the trust that he has lost as a result of his deception. Like the apostle Paul, who lost trust in John Mark for a time but ultimately learned to trust him again, so you can learn to trust your husband if he proves himself to be a teller of the truth.

"I cannot continue to live in this constant state of
confusion that this marriage keeps me in."

RELATED SCRIPTURE: 2 Cor. 4:8; 1 Cor. 10: 13; Phil. 4:13

The apostle Paul sometimes found himself in perplexing situations. He didn't always understand what God was up to in every circumstance. He didn't always know how to interpret the specifics of his trials and, therefore, was somewhat limited at times in knowing exactly how to respond to them. But although he was *perplexed*, he did not *despair* because he knew enough about God's attributes (e.g., sovereignty, goodness, faithfulness) that he could trust God to work out everything for His glory and Paul's own ultimate good (see 2 Cor. 4:8).

He may have been, as the Greek New Testament words imply, "at a loss" to explain what was happening but not "totally at a loss" so as to lose hope. Paul may not have known with certainty what was going to happen next, but he certainly knew that God was in his circumstances, working all things according to His predetermined plan (cf. Acts 2:23).

That's the secret of finding hope. One's ability to find hope in a seemingly hopeless situation is directly related to the ability to see God's hand in that situation. If you are despairing as a result of your troubled marriage, you are probably not focusing on what God intends to do in your life, and for His kingdom as a result of it.

"I've lived with her for umpteen years, and I know that she will never change."

RELATED SCRIPTURE: Ps. 138:8; 1 Cor. 1:8; Eph. 3:20; Phil. 1:6; 2:13; 2 Tim. 1:12; Jude 24

You are not a prophet or the son of a prophet, so you shouldn't be making prophecies about the future. When you think about the future of your believing wife, you ought to believe what the Bible says in a dozen ways about it—namely, that the Lord will perfect that which concerns her. Besides, there are trained counselors all around the country who are committed to helping people make those changes biblically.[12]

"My family and friends are all advising me to get out of this horrible marriage."

RELATED SCRIPTURE: Prov. 11:14; 15:22; 24:6; Rom. 14:22–23; 1 Cor. 15:33

12. You may find a biblical counselor in your area by visiting the website of the National Association of Nouthetic Counselors, https://www.nanc.org, or by calling NANC at (317) 337-9100.

I know of at least *one* concerned individual who is *not* advising you to leave—and *my* advice is based on the Bible. Can you say that about your other counselors? Have your other counselors been able to support their counsel with solid biblical support as I have been doing in this booklet? In the multitude of godly counselors there is safety. In the multitude of ungodly ones there is confusion.[13]

I cannot cover in this limited space the dozens of other excuses I've heard hopeless people use to justify their desire to employ sinful means of extricating themselves from difficult marriages. Having tried solution after solution to no avail, they select the only option they believe is left that will end their misery—terminating the marriage.

My job as a biblical counselor is twofold. The first task is to help the married couple understand that in the final analysis, the misery they will experience on the other side of a sinful divorce will exceed the misery they will experience if they, in dependence on God's grace, choose to fully put His solutions into practice. Second is to help them see that there are, in fact, other solutions (God's) that they either have not considered or have not fully implemented.

If you are truly a Christian, by abandoning your first love,[14] you have been grieving (and quite possibly quenching) the Spirit of God, who has been given to you for your help and comfort. He stands ready "to will and to work for [to make you

13. Scripture encourages us to seek counsel from a multitude of counselors not because the Bible is insufficient to guide us and we therefore need a bit of human wisdom to supplement what the Bible says. Rather, seeking counsel from a multitude of people who know the Scriptures will help ensure that we are getting a more complete understanding of what the Bible says about the matter. One counselor makes his point from the Sermon on the Mount. Another shows you an additional guiding principle from one of the General Epistles. A third basically agrees with the first two but points out a balancing truth from the Proverbs. When you put it all together, you have assurance that you will be able to make a well-informed, biblically based decision. Are you really that confident about this divorce you are contemplating?

14. Your first love should be the Lord Jesus (cf. Rev. 2:4); your second love should be your spouse (cf. Gen. 2:24; Eph. 5:28–30).

willing and able to do] His good pleasure" (Phil. 2:13). But there is a catch. You must first, in dependence on Him, be *willing* to work out your salvation with fear and trembling (Phil. 2:12). And I pray that you are trembling right now—especially as you consider how serious a matter dumping your spouse is in "the eyes of Him with whom we have to do" (Heb. 4:13). Indeed, "it is a terrifying thing to fall into the hands of the living God" (Heb. 10:31). And now that you have read this booklet, your judgment is likely to be even greater if you harden your heart even further by rejecting the truth to which you have just been exposed.

And just in case I haven't convinced you that your suffering will be greater if you disobediently divorce, let me ask you one final question: Why are you unwilling to suffer for the Lord? Suffering for doing what is right is part of your calling as a Christian.

> For to you it has been granted for Christ's sake, not only to believe in Him, but also to suffer for His sake. (Phil. 1:29)

> For you have been called for this purpose, since Christ also suffered for you, leaving you an example for you to follow in His steps, who committed no sin, nor was any deceit found in His mouth; and while being reviled, He did not revile in return; while suffering, He uttered no threats, but kept entrusting Himself to Him who judges righteously; and He Himself bore our sins in His body on the cross, so that we might die to sin and live to righteousness; for by His wounds you were healed. (1 Peter 2:21–24)

Don't be a coward. If you have the courage to sign those divorce documents, have the courage to answer this question first: Why are you unwilling to suffer for the One who suffered so much for you?

Well, that's about it. Thank you again for taking the time to hear my plea and for bearing with the straightforward manner in which I have spoken. I pray that I have given you pause to rethink your decision.

Chances are that the difficulties you are going through that are tempting you to throw in the towel on your marriage are *not* nearly as intolerable as you have imagined. "You have not yet resisted to the point of shedding blood in your striving against sin" (Heb. 12:4). Your selfish discontentment is exaggerating your troubles in your mind. Sure, they are painful, but let me exhort you one more time not to feel a flesh wound as though it were a knife through your heart. The truth is, if you proceed with an unbiblical divorce, *you* will be the one putting the knife through the heart of God and yet another nail in the hand of your Lord and Savior, Jesus Christ.

Appendix: Torn Between Two Lovers?

Perhaps the greatest reason you are wanting out of your marriage is that you have "fallen in love" with someone other than your spouse. If so, there is hope for your situation. Many unfaithful spouses I've counseled over the past twenty-three years wondered two things:

- "Can I ever get over these powerful feelings I have toward the other woman/man?"
- "Will I ever be able to love my spouse with the same kind of intensity I have for the other person?"

If you are a Christian who is truly willing to do what the Bible says, the answer to both of these questions is *yes*.

When you met and married your spouse, you, in effect, opened up a lifetime savings account at a brand-new bank: First National _____ (insert the name of your spouse). You soon began to make some rather large investments in that account. You invested a good deal of time, effort, thought, money, and even your own body. You also placed in the safety deposit box of that bank many of your valuables, along with the majority of your secret treasures. And for a while, perhaps a good long while, you were pleased with the interest you received on your investments.

Then, little by little, after becoming disillusioned with the returns you were receiving on your principal, you slowed down the frequency with which you deposited your assets. Perhaps you even stopped making new investments and simply tried to live off the interest for a while.

Then one day, you received information quite unexpectedly about a brand-new bank that had just opened a branch close to where you work (or golf, or play tennis): First Federal _____ (insert the name of the other person to whom you gave your heart or body). This new bank promised to give you a much better return on your investments—especially in those areas in which the other bank had disappointed you.

You began investigating all the additional perks that First Federal had to offer. The list seemed quite impressive. So before you knew what you were doing (and before you counted the costs), you opened up a First Federal account—you signed on the dotted line without carefully reading the fine print. Little by little, you began making additional deposits in this new bank. It wasn't long before you were taking your assets out of First National and moving them to First Federal. First National, on more than one occasion, brought to your attention the indisputable fact that your principal investment with it was dwindling considerably. Of course, you denied it and tried to shift the blame back to First National. But deep down in your heart, you knew who was really at fault.

For a while, it helped to remind yourself that First National wasn't quite as good a deal as you thought it would be when you opened up your first account there. You had convinced yourself long ago that First National would probably never be able to provide you with the returns you were looking for.

But be that as it may, now you're in a real quandary. It's as Jesus said it would be: "Where your treasure is, there your heart will be also" (Matt. 6:21). You now have investments in both banks, and consequently, your heart is torn between the two of them—you have feelings for both.

So what are you going to do? If you want God's best (and if you want the answers to those two questions I raised at the beginning of this appendix to be *yes*), you will have to take two very important steps.

1. Totally close the account at First Federal.
2. Systematically redeposit every last investment that was made in First Federal back into First National.

You must completely end the adulterous affair. This other person must be plainly told that the relationship is over. If possible, ask for forgiveness (preferably on a conference call with your spouse or pastor on the line) for your selfishness and deceit. There can be no continuing communication (no secret rendezvous, telephone calls, cards, letters, or e-mails). The other person should be emphatically told not to contact you anymore. You must be willing to amputate from your life anything that will tempt you to reopen this illegal bank account.

Jesus, after explaining to the disciples that lusting for a woman was adultery of the heart, said this to His disciples:

> If your right eye makes you stumble, tear it out and throw it from you; for it is better for you to lose one of the parts of your body, than for your whole body to be thrown into hell. If your right hand makes you stumble, cut it off and throw it from you; for it is better for you to lose one of the parts of your body, than for your whole body to go into hell. (Matt. 5:29–30)

He told them that they must remove anything from their lives that made them stumble into sin—even something they cherished (cf. Eph. 5:29). Don't keep any mementos, photographs, keepsakes, or other memorabilia that might tempt you to spend time thinking about (and fueling romantic feelings for) the other person. You may have to change your telephone number, your e-mail address, or the route you take to and from the office. I've known several men and women who were even willing to give up their jobs in order to take this important step.

Having closed the illegal account, you must next begin the process of systematically transferring all your assets back to the original bank. Exactly how much of your money, time, thoughts, dreams, affection, initiative, and creative energies did you invest in the account with the other person? They will all have to be reinvested with your spouse. Did you buy the other person gifts? Ask yourself, "What kind of gifts can I buy for my spouse?" Did you go on dates with the other person? Ask yourself, "Where can I take my spouse out for a date?" Did you call the other person from or at work? Ask, "When are the best times for me to surprise my spouse with a telephone call?" How many hours did you spend thinking about what you could do to please the other person? Spend that much time thinking about what you can do to adore and please your spouse. And perhaps most importantly, how much time did you spend revealing your heart to the other person and listening intently as he or she revealed his or her heart to you? Invest the same amount of time in the revelation process with your spouse. Are you willing to invest the effort and creativity necessary to make these kinds of redeposits? If you're serious about obeying God, you will be willing to invest whatever it takes to repair your marriage. Like Zaccheus (Luke 19:8–10), you reveal the sincerity of your repentance by your willingness to make restitution.

If you want your feelings to change, you must begin to court your spouse as vigorously as you courted the other person. After they've changed, continue courting him or her "as long as you both shall live."

"Okay, I see what you are saying, but when I think of all those promises I made to the other person—for the most part with every intention of keeping them—I feel so guilty."

The fact that you feel guilty is probably a *good* thing. It means you've not yet totally defiled your conscience. Not unlike a computer virus, your sin may have simply misprogrammed your conscience to believe that you owe the other person more than you really do. But you are more indebted to your spouse than you are to the other adulterer. You owe God even more than that. You may have made promises[1] to the other person that you must ask forgiveness for breaking. But breaking your vow to God and lifetime covenant with your spouse will have further-reaching consequences than breaking a rash promise to your adulterous lover (cf. Eccl. 5:1–7).

"But I can't just abandon her. That wouldn't be Christian!"

Closing the bank account is not abandonment. Your pastor or another biblical counselor is in a much better position to minister to the other person than you are. If you are truly concerned about the welfare of the other individual, turn him or her over to the care of a pastor or other biblical counselor. You are not qualified to help in this situation. The other person has also sinned and may be in need of repentance. Don't stand in the way of divine discipline by trying to remove the culpability and consequences of his or her sin (cf. Heb. 12:1–11).

> Do not be deceived, God is not mocked; for whatever a man sows, this he will also reap. For the one who sows to his own flesh will from the flesh reap corruption, but the one who sows to the Spirit will from the Spirit reap eternal life. Let us not lose heart in doing good, for in due time we will reap if we do not grow weary. So then, while we have opportunity, let us do good to all people, and especially to those who are of the household of the faith. (Gal. 6:7–10)

If you are willing to take these two steps, then you will be well on your way to saving your marriage. If you are not

---

1. See Proverbs 6:1–5 for general instructions about what to do when you make a foolish promise.

willing, as much as is possible, to close First Federal and reinvest in First National, it is doubtful that you will ever fully "fall out of love" with your adulterous lover. May God grant you the humility, courage, and grace to make the right choice.